GUN CRIME

Dirk Flint

W
FRANKLIN WATTS
LONDON·SYDNEY

First published in 2011 by
Franklin Watts
338 Euston Road
London NW1 3BH

Franklin Watts Australia
Level 17/207 Kent Street
Sydney NSW 2000

Series editor: Jeremy Smith
Editors: Julia Bird
Design: sprout.uk.com
Artworks: sprout.uk.com
Picture researcher: Diana Morris

A CIP catalogue record for this book is available
from the British Library.

ISBN 978 0 7496 9585 9

Dewey classification: 364.1

Printed in China

Franklin Watts is a division of Hachette Children's
Books, an Hachette UK company.
www.hachette.co.uk

Picture credits: Ace Stock Ltd/Alamy: front cover b.
Action Press/Rex Features: 16. Allstar PL/Alamy:
39b. AP/PAI: 10, 11. Austral Int/Rex Features: 40.
Julien Behal/PA Wire/PAI: 14.Bettmann/Corbis: 8.
Ashley Cooper/Alamy: 28. Anthony Devlin/PA Wire/
PAI: 15tr. Bill Gadbury /Shutterstock: 15tl. Getty
Images: 36. Greg Goodman/Shutterstock: front
cover t. Johnny Green/PA Archive/PAI: 37. Themba
Hadebe/AP/PAI: 24. haveseen/Shutterstock: front
cover c, 5. KPA/Zuma/Rex Features: 35. Jose Luis
Magana/AP/PAI: 27t. John McLellan/Rex Features:
21. Met Police/AP/Topfoto: 29. Kevin Moroney/
Aurora Photos/Alamy: 13b. Martin Moxter/
Imagebroker/Alamy: 39t. National Pictures/Topfoto:
30, 41. NewsPictures/MCP/Rex Features: 12.
OJO Images/Rex Features: 9. PA/PAI: 22br.
Photos 12/Alamy: 38. Rex Features: 17, 25, 27b.
Martin Smith-Rodden/AP/PAI: 33. Thomas
Sbampato/Imagebroker/Alamy: 19. Martin H Simon/
Corbis: 32. Sipa Press/Rex Features: 18, 23, 26, 31.
Steve Starr/Corbis: 34. Mark St George/Rex
Features: 22bl. Jason Stitt/istockphoto: 13t.
Mark J Terrill/AP/PAI: 20.

Every attempt has been made to clear copyright.
Should there be any inadvertent omission please
apply to the publisher for rectification.

CONTENTS

GUN CRIME –
OUT OF CONTROL?

In many parts of the world, violent crime is on the increase. Read the papers and barely a week goes by when there isn't a headline about a gangland shooting, armed robbery or the seizure of illegal guns by police officers or customs officials. Can anything be done to control such gun crime, and should there be tougher laws on owning a gun?

The right to bear arms

In countries such as the United States of America, the debate about gun ownership has gone on for hundreds of years. In 1791, the US Bill of Rights declared the 'right of the people to keep and bear arms', and when the state of Georgia tried to ban handguns in 1837, the law was thrown out. In the late 1930s, the United Kingdom and the United States both passed laws requiring gun owners to have a licence, and banning the sale of weapons to convicted criminals. These laws were poorly enforced, however, and it was only after the shooting of US President John F. Kennedy in 1963 that the United States clamped down on sales of firearms.

▼ *President John F. Kennedy riding with his wife Jacqueline in a motorcade in Dallas, Texas, on 22 November, 1963. Moments later, Kennedy was shot by an assassin. Kennedy is just one of four US presidents to be assassinated by gunmen.*

Fewer guns, fewer deaths?

Despite tighter controls on the sale of weapons, the argument continues to rage over the link between guns and violent crimes such as murder and armed robbery. One view is that the high murder rate in the United States is a direct result of the fact that so many Americans own firearms. If there were fewer guns there would be fewer deaths. Others argue that guns can protect innocent people from violence and actually prevent crime: if a robber walks into a shop and the owner produces a weapon, the robber will think twice about committing a crime.

▲ *It is sometimes said that guns don't kill, people do. However, there is an undeniable link between gun ownership and deaths caused by shooting.*

Around the world

While the problem of gun crime is bad in the United States, it is even more of an issue in some South American countries, where it is linked to the powerful and lucrative drugs trade (see page 11). Gun deaths are also on the increase in countries such as Russia, Ireland and Australia.

WHAT IS GUN CRIME?

Gun crime is any violence or crime carried out with a firearm. Put simply, guns kill. If someone assaults you with a knife, you are five times less likely to die than if you are shot. Even if robbers do not intend to harm their victims, a bank robbery can turn into a fatal shooting if they panic and fire.

The rise of gun violence

Although pistols were invented in the 16th century, guns weren't much used until the 20th century. In 1904, there were just four armed robberies in the whole of London. One reason is that people weren't used to handling guns until the First World War (1914–1918), when millions of men were drafted into the army. The introduction of mass production also meant that guns were much more readily available in the 20th century. The 1920s saw the dramatic use of machine guns by mobsters in US cities such as Chicago, and the majority of gun crime today is still linked to criminal gangs.

Deliberate or accidental?

Some gun crimes are deliberate. But guns can also lead to unplanned deaths. These types of shootings often involve people who are known to each other. In the heat of an argument, one may pull out a gun and finish the row. Often a husband kills a wife in this way or a young man kills a friend or parent. Children who come across a weapon in the house may fire it

▶ Legendary gangster Al Capone lived by the gun. The Chicago mobster was probably behind the Saint Valentine's Day Massacre on 14 February 1929, when seven men were brutally gunned down in a Chicago garage.

▲ Police investigate a shooting in the Mexican border town of Ciudad Juárez. The city is a major battle ground for drug cartels and 5,000 people have been murdered there since 2006, earning it the name of 'the most violent city on Earth'.

accidentally. Some gun violence statistics include self-inflicted injuries – suicide victims often use a gun. Suicides account for almost half of the 30,000 gun deaths in the United States each year, while accidental gun deaths account for another 700.

Lethal weapon

Because guns are so deadly, the police take gun crimes very seriously. In the United Kingdom, gun crime is seen as one of the most troubling types of criminal activity. Yet gun crime in Europe is actually rare compared to that in countries like Colombia and Mexico, where an all-out war between the police and rival drug gangs has led to a string of bloody gunfights and brutal murders, along with a rash of gun-factory raids and smuggling busts.

FACT FILE

Gun crime is often linked to poverty. Most studies reveal you are more likely to be shot in a deprived neighbourhood. However, crime has many causes, including culture. Japan has a very low rate of gun crime: in 2006 there were just 53 shootings in a population of over 127 million. Japan has tight gun controls, but the low gun crime rate is probably due to the fact that in Japanese culture it is very important to conform and respect your fellow citizens.

WHAT GUNS ARE USED?

Since the 1960s, the kinds of weapons used in murders and violent crime haven't changed all that much. While rifles and shotguns account for 15% of all homicides, more than half of all murders are carried out with handguns, probably due to the fact that they are easier to conceal and buy illegally.

Criminals and guns

All guns use gunpowder to blast a bullet out of a barrel at high speed and with deadly force. The most lethal are automatic weapons and machine guns that can hold and fire a large number of rounds (bullets) very quickly. Criminal gangs in many countries now use weapons like these in battles with rival gangs and the police. Other long-barrelled weapons include shotguns, which are devastating at close range. Criminals often saw off part of the barrel to make them easier to carry and conceal. Hunting rifles can fire a single shot accurately over a long distance. They are typically used by assassins and serial killers rather than in street crimes.

▼ *Two armed gang members at a drug selling point in Rio de Janeiro, Brazil. The man on the left is carrying an automatic rifle. This deadly weapon is capable of firing lots of bullets in quick succession.*

◀ *Handguns such as this pistol are a favourite among street gangs as they are cheap, simple to use and easily hidden.*

Heavy weapons

Terrorist groups often set out to kill as many people as possible, so they are more likely to be armed with heavy weapons such as assault rifles and heavy machine guns. In the past, terrorists have also used weapons such as the Glock plastic gun, which could pass through a metal detector. However, since the 2001 attacks on the World Trade Center and US Pentagon there has been much tighter security at airports.

Automatics

Automatic weapons and shotguns may be more deadly, but street criminals, especially young gang members, often prefer semi-automatic pistols because of their looks and the fact that they can hold 10 or more rounds. Because of their size, these pistols are also easy to hide. The cheapest can be bought for under £80 on the black market in the UK, and are even cheaper in the United States.

▼ *Most guns are made of metal and show up on the X-ray machines and metal detectors used by airport security.*

ON TARGET

Most countries have much stricter laws controlling handguns than sporting rifles because of how they are used. Handguns were banned in the United Kingdom after the Dunblane school massacre in 1996. It is still illegal for pistol shooters to train anywhere in Britain, though the government has given various shooting events the go-ahead in the 2012 Olympics. Britain's Olympic shooting hopefuls have to travel to Switzerland to train for their events.

WHO COMMITS GUN CRIMES?

Many people who carry guns set out to kill or hurt others, such as hitmen working for a drug gang or a paid assassin. Guns are also weapons of terror: kidnappers and robbers use them to scare other people into handing over money or valuables. The danger is that as violent crime increases, more people will also buy guns to protect themselves, leading to more accidental shootings and deaths.

▲ Kidnappers and other criminals use guns to intimidate their victims and keep them under control.

Why carry a gun?

A gun offers criminals several advantages over weapons such as knives. With a gun in their hand robbers can keep their distance, making it easier to make a getaway and harder for a victim to fight back. Guns also give criminals a psychological advantage. It's much easier to control a bank full of staff, for example, with a gun than with a knife. For others, guns are a form of protection and security. Whatever the reason, if someone can get their hands on a gun when they lose their temper or panic, they're far more likely to kill someone else.

Men and guns

Some people, more often men, become obsessed with guns. Some are just enthusiasts who enjoy polishing their weapons, firing them at a shooting range, or hunting. Other men like the feeling of power a gun gives them. Some experts say hormones such as testosterone make men naturally more aggressive.

◄ *Many young boys enjoy playing with toy or replica guns.*

Gangland violence

In many countries, criminal gangs are responsible for the majority of gun crime. A small incident can quickly lead to all-out war. A bloody battle between Jamaican gangs broke out after a pair of sunglasses was stolen. A deadly gangland feud in the city of Limerick, Ireland started in the early 2000s after a fight in a school playground resulted in a schoolgirl getting her face slashed. The violence quickly escalated, and in November 2000 gunmen pumped a rival gang member full of bullets in a crowded bar. Since then there have been over 15 gun deaths linked to the feud.

Others argue that boys are often taught to be tough or aggressive. Whatever the reason, men are usually the ones who use guns. Worldwide around 90% of all robberies and violent attacks are carried out by men.

ON TARGET

There is a growing trend in the United States and the United Kingdom for teenage girls to get dragged into the gun culture by hiding weapons for their criminal boyfriends or relatives. To combat this, the Metropolitan Police launched a TV campaign in September 2009. This warned young women that storing weapons for gangsters could lead to a prison sentence. During 2008–9, over 25 women were arrested in London for storing weapons, including several teenagers. One 16-year-old was found with a loaded pistol in her bedroom.

▶ *Though most armed criminals are men, female friends and relatives can get caught up in violent crime by hiding their weapons for them.*

CASE STUDY: KILLING SPREES

Some kinds of gun crime are particularly hard for the police to combat. Mass murderers can go on a killing 'spree' with little or no warning, and several gun massacres have been carried out by teenagers with no previous criminal record.

Student massacres

Gun massacres have taken place in many parts of the world, but are particularly common in schools and colleges. On 1 August 1966, Charles Joseph Whitman, a student at the University of Texas in Austin, USA, shot dead 14 people and wounded 32 at the university campus in the first known killing spree of its kind. More recently, on 11 March 2009 gunman 17-year-old Tim Kretschmer went on a shooting spree at his old secondary school in Winnenden, Germany and at a local car dealership. He killed 15 people before turning the gun on himself.

Columbine

Perhaps the most notorious school massacre took place in 1999, when two US students, 18-year-old Dylan Klebold and 17-year-old Eric Harris, went on the rampage at Columbine High School in Littleton, Colorado, USA. In the months before the massacre, they had managed to buy two handguns, two shotguns and a semiautomatic rifle, as well as ammunition and explosives.

▼ *Local people leave floral tributes near the school in Winnenden where Tim Kretschmer killed nine students and one teacher.*

On the morning of 20 April, Klebold and Harris entered the school cafeteria and planted bombs hidden inside duffel bags. They went back to their cars, but when the bombs failed to explode, they armed themselves and walked back to the school. In just 15 minutes, they shot and killed 12 students and a teacher, and injured another 21 pupils before killing themselves.

Because the two shooters committed suicide, it was hard to know what their motives were and whether anything could have been done to stop them. A report by the FBI argued that both students had mental health problems. Other experts blamed video games and films or debated whether Klebold and Harris were bullied at school.

▼ *Eric Harris and Dylan Klebold caught on CCTV in the cafeteria during their killing spree at Columbine High School on 20 April 1999. One of the most frightening aspects of the tragedy was how easily the pair got hold of firearms.*

ON TARGET

What can be done to prevent school massacres?

• Most attacks happen so suddenly and quickly that armed police units only arrive after they have finished. That said, police units in some countries are now trained to stop the shooter at all costs, to stop him from killing more.

• In the United States, many university campuses now have electronic devices that can lock doors or send emergency emails and phone messages. Many schools have evacuation drills in case of an emergency.

• Some colleges have programmes that try to identify and provide treatment for students who might pose a risk. However, a US Secret Service study showed that shooters come from many different backgrounds. Most were not misfits and had no history of violence.

• More controversial are calls that students should be allowed to carry guns so that they can protect themselves. Many worry this could lead to accidental deaths.

HOW MUCH GUN CRIME IS THERE?

The amount of gun crime can vary a great deal from country to country. It is particularly high in places where organised crime or drug gangs are very powerful (see p.11). Gun crime is also more common in countries such as South Africa where there is a big divide between rich and poor. Almost everywhere, violent crime is higher in big cities as this is where gangs are usually based.

▲ The police in countries such as Colombia where drug-related killings are a big problem have to be extra vigilant. Here, Colombian police are checking bus passengers at a roadblock for weapons and drugs.

Low levels

In most developed countries such as the UK, the overall level of gun crime is generally very low. Over the last ten years, between 40 and 100 people have been killed each year by firearms in the UK, with around 20,000 incidents each year involving guns. While very frightening for the victims, most did not result in injury. In fact, in recent years, four times more people were killed by knives than by guns in the United Kingdom. This may be due in part to the UK's strict laws on gun ownership, as few ordinary citizens have access to guns.

A gun culture?

In contrast, gun crime is high in the United States, where a quarter of robberies are carried out with guns. Here around 12,000 people are shot every year – accounting for more than two out of every three killings. That's an average of 33 people every day.

Some blame the gun culture in the United States, where it is relatively easy to buy a gun. In most US states, as long as you are 21 and have no criminal record, you simply need a driver's licence or some other form of ID to buy a pistol legally. John Hinkley, the man who tried to kill US President Ronald Reagan, used forged ID papers and paid only $27 (around £18) for the gun he used. Around 40 per cent of American households own a gun, usually for self-defence. Unfortunately, this leads to around 700 to 800 accidental deaths each year.

▼ Many US citizens defend their right to carry weapons, especially in wilderness areas such as Alaska where hunting is popular. Problems arise when these guns get into the hands of children or people with mental health problems.

BUSTED!

One of the arguments in favour of people owning guns in the United States is the fact that firearms can be used in self-defence or to stop a crime. In January 2002, for example, two students at the Appalachian School of Law in Grundy, Virginia, ran to their cars and took out their pistols after hearing gunfire. They used them to disarm a shooter who had already killed three people, including the Dean of the school, and wounded three more. Some have used the case to lead calls for teachers and students at educational institutions to be allowed to arm themselves.

GETTING HOLD OF GUNS

A determined criminal usually has no problem getting hold of a gun. In the United States guns are freely available at gun shows, pawn shops and flea markets. In the United Kingdom, firearms are smuggled in from countries with more relaxed gun laws, and sold on the black market or the Internet. If all else fails, weapons can be stolen – around 500,000 guns are stolen every year in the United States.

Freely available

It can be very hard for the police to stop criminals getting guns. Seung-Hui Cho, a student who went on an armed rampage at Virginia Tech in the United States in April 2007, simply ordered a gun on the Internet and picked it up from a local pawn shop. Although pistols, shotguns and rifles can be bought legally from stores in the US, criminals prefer to buy weapons on the black market so they are harder to trace. For example, a popular gang weapon is the Russian SKS assault rifle. Even a very powerful weapon like this may only cost about US $100 (around £68). Gun traffickers like to peddle handguns to gang members because they buy them at such rock-bottom prices that they can tack on a hefty mark-up and still sell them on cheaply.

◄ *Although local authorities often try to ban gun shows such as this one in Pomona, California, USA, they remain extremely popular.*

Drugs and guns

The trade in guns is often linked to other crimes. Drug addicts who burgle homes can trade stolen guns for drugs, for example. The drug dealer then sells the guns on to criminals such as carjackers and robbers. Though firearms manufacturers are required by law to put serial numbers on guns, it is very hard to track a gun once it has entered this second-hand market.

▼ *Former army sergeant Paul Alexander, shown here in police custody, supplied weapons to criminal gangs that were linked to 28 firearms crimes in the UK.*

BUSTED!

For some, dealing in death is a highly profitable business. Former British soldier Paul Alexander ran a secret gun factory and supplied feuding gangs with assassination kits and other weapons linked to a murder, four attempted murders and an armed robbery. Each kit cost £1,500 and contained a handgun, silencer and three or four magazines with up to 11 rounds in them. The police finally swooped on Alexander after his DNA was discovered on a handgun seized two years before. The barn where he worked contained 12,000 gun parts and 28 guns and rifles.

CONTROLS AND PENALTIES

Guns make it easy to kill, so in most developed countries there are strict controls on owning or buying a gun. In the United Kingdom you need a licence to own a shotgun or rifle, while handguns are banned. However, gun control laws differ widely from one country to another. Despite the various arguments, countries with fewer guns do tend to have fewer gun crimes.

Self-defence

In the United States, gun-rights groups argue that people have a right to defend themselves. In Britain, a person may use 'reasonable force' to protect themselves or others or prevent a crime. But what is reasonable force? In the United States, a householder can shoot an intruder if his or her life is threatened. This is known as justifiable homicide and the person who shoots an intruder is not charged with any crime.

In Britain, people have been sent to jail for shooting intruders. The most well-known case is Tony Martin. In 1999, this Norfolk farmer shot dead an intruder in his home. He was jailed for life for murder, but after an appeal his sentence was reduced to three years.

For and against

Gun-rights groups claim that guns kept in a house can often be used to scare a robber or intruder away without needing to fire a shot. On the other hand, those in favour of gun control point to the fact that a gun in a home is far more likely to result in injury or death for someone living there. The spread of guns also breeds fear: in a survey carried out in 2005 almost 40% of the US teenagers interviewed believed they would be shot at some point in their lives, and the same percentage felt gun violence could break out in their school.

▼ *Norfolk farmer Tony Martin (left) became a focus of huge debate in the UK after shooting dead a teenager who was burgling his home and wounding another, Brendan Fearon (right).*

▲ *Though China's weapon laws are very strict, gun crime is still a major problem. Here police officers in the city of Xi'an, China, burn confiscated illegal and fake guns during a campaign to destroy illegal weapons.*

Tougher penalties

US gun-rights groups blame criminals for the rise in gun crime. They believe the best way to reduce it is to introduce tougher penalties for criminals. China's weapons laws are among the world's toughest. Private individuals are banned from owning rifles, pistols and even gun replicas. Possession of a single gun can lead to a prison sentence as long as three years, and the penalty for a gun crime is often execution. In September 2007 a young man was found guilty of using a replica gun to rob a bank customer of US$218,000 (£150,000) and was given a 19-year prison sentence. Yet a gun culture is still taking hold in China and the police face increasingly well-armed and aggressive criminals, so perhaps tough penalties are not the deterrent they appear.

FACT FILE

Maximum penalty for possession of an illegal weapon around the world:

- US – varies; up to ten years in prison

- UK – ten years in prison

- Canada – five years in prison

- Mexico – 30 years in prison

- Japan – ten years in prison and one million yen fine (around £7,350).

ARMING THE POLICE

How do you deal with armed criminals? Most police forces have special military-style units equipped with assault rifles, stun grenades and even armoured personnel carriers. By the time these specialist teams arrive on the scene, however, it may be too late; so in many forces all police officers carry guns.

Visible security

Most countries in Europe and North America routinely arm police officers in the belief that guns are needed to protect the police and the public against a growing number of armed criminals. There is also the argument that people feel safer when they see armed police. For example, after the 9/11 terrorist attacks on New York, police officers at British airports started carrying sub-machine guns. These would not necessarily make a big difference in an attack, but they are a lot more visible than pistols or other light arms.

BUSTED!

Officers from the Metropolitan Police's famous Flying Squad deal with armed robbery and are regularly armed themselves. In November 2000 an armed gang set out to rob the Millennium Star diamond and other jewels worth over £350 million from London's Millennium Dome. The robbers planned to smash their way into the Dome, then escape up the River Thames in a speedboat. After a tip-off, officers from the Flying Squad disguised themselves as cleaners, hid their weapons in bin bags and lay in wait. After the gang rammed the Dome with a stolen digger, the armed police swooped and quickly overpowered them.

▶ *South Africa has one of the highest violent crime rates in the world, so during the 2010 World Cup, the world's top football teams were escorted by armed police to and from the airports.*

Specialist units

Almost every police force has specialist units that deal with armed criminals. Such units may prevent shoot-outs, as the threat of force is enough to make many armed gangs surrender. However, though these officers are highly trained, innocent people still get shot, either by mistake due to inaccurate information, or because they get caught in the crossfire of a shoot-out. In March 2006, an unarmed doctor was shot and killed by a Special Weapons and Tactics (SWAT) force in the state of Virginia, USA. On 22 July 2005, a police anti-terrorist unit wrongly identified Brazilian Jean Charles De Menezes as a suicide bomber on the London Underground and shot him dead at close range. Many people were shocked that the British police had a shoot-to-kill policy.

Guns on the beat

Most British police on the beat are not armed. The theory behind this is that once a police officer has a gun, they may be tempted to use their weapon rather than relying on less deadly options to stop a criminal, such as stun guns, CS gas or simply talking them into surrendering. If police are not armed, some criminals may choose not to arm themselves too. They also know that using a weapon in a robbery will lead to a much tougher sentence if they are caught.

▼ *CCTV images captured the last movements of 27-year- old Brazilian, Jean Charles de Menezes, shortly before he was shot dead by anti-terrorist police at Stockwell Underground station on 22 July 2005.*

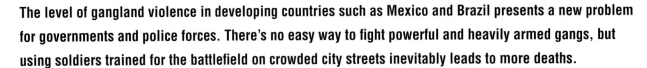

WAR ON THE STREETS

The level of gangland violence in developing countries such as Mexico and Brazil presents a new problem for governments and police forces. There's no easy way to fight powerful and heavily armed gangs, but using soldiers trained for the battlefield on crowded city streets inevitably leads to more deaths.

Slum violence

In Brazil, 50,000 people are murdered each year. Many deaths occur in slums known as favelas. Many of these slums are controlled by illegal armed groups, drug traffickers or vigilante militias. Each week in the big Brazilian cities of Sao Paolo and Rio de Janeiro, the newspapers are filled with pictures of bulletproof vehicles and gun-battles between drug gangs. In Sao Paolo, the police concentrate their attacks on drug gangs, while trying to improve the living conditions within the favelas. In Rio, however, the police battle gangs head-on – armed units go into the favelas with guns blazing, then occupy whole blocks for weeks or months. In 2009, around 1,000 people were killed in such police operations, including innocent bystanders.

Trigger-happy police?

Brazil is not the only country where such extreme tactics are used. In Venezuela, police officers gun down an estimated 900 people every year. For every officer killed in a shoot-out, 39 suspects die. In Colombia during the early 2000s, 'death squads' made up of off-duty soldiers and policemen patrolled the streets at night and each year gunned down thousands of government opponents.

▼ *Military officers keep guard on top of a slum house during an operation in the Rocinha favela in Rio de Janeiro, Brazil. In an attempt to stop bloody wars between rival drug gangs, the Brazilian police forces sometimes occupy such slums for many months.*

A war on drugs

At the start of 2007, Mexican President Felipe Calderon declared war on drug traffickers, involving a force of around 45,000 troops and 5,000 police officers. So far, around 11,000 people have died, many in bloody shootouts and assassinations. Some were innocent bystanders who got caught in the crossfire. In the border city of Ciudad Juárez, police pickups and military trucks packed with heavily armed troops constantly patrol the streets. In February 2009, the city's police chief quit after several officers were shot dead and signs appeared threatening that more would be killed unless he stepped down. Three years on, the war is far from won, and the bloodshed continues.

◀ *Felipe Calderon was elected President of Mexico in December 2006. He has vowed to take apart Mexico's powerful drug cartels as part of his election campaign.*

▼ *In 2008, police in Washington, DC attempted to tackle rising gun crime in the Trinidad neighbourhood by creating a 'Neighborhood Safety Zone'. Police stopped cars at checkpoints on roads into the district. If drivers didn't have a good enough reason to be in the neighbourhood, they were turned back.*

ON TARGET

In the neighbourhood of Trinidad, Washington DC, USA, police checkpoints have been used to control trouble hotspots following a rise in gun murders. This 'occupation' style of policing follows methods developed by the Israeli police in Palestine. However, although roadblocks may make life difficult for armed criminals, they also make locals feel as if they are living in a police state where they are constantly being watched.

SOLVING GUN CRIME

Guns are deadly weapons, but they can also provide a trail of clues linking the victim, the weapon and the shooter. Police officers arriving at the main crime scene interview witnesses and carefully record and collect every possible scrap of evidence. It is a long, complicated and often tedious job – but one tiny bloodstain or fingerprint can unlock the whole case.

At the crime scene

The main crime scene is where the shooting took place, though sometimes the victim's body or the gun are found elsewhere and these also become crime scenes. Arriving at the scene, police officers will try to arrest the shooter and help any victims who are still alive. Their next job is to secure the crime scene. This means making sure that everything remains exactly the way it was when the crime happened.

The whole crime scene is then recorded with photos and sketches. Meanwhile, detectives take the names and addresses of witnesses and may ask them a few key questions, such as how many shots were fired. Finally, the crime scene investigators (CSI) get down to the nitty gritty of collecting evidence. Great care is taken – if they're scraping a sample of blood from a window for example, they must make sure they don't accidentally wipe off any fingerprints at the same time.

▲ Forensics experts sift a crime scene looking for potential clues near the River Kent in Cumbria, England. They wear disposable cover-alls to avoid contaminating the evidence.

▲ Although CCTV cameras can help investigators to track down criminals, hardened criminals can work their way around the surveillance by preventing the camera from getting a good shot of their face (in this case the criminal is wearing a motorcycle helmet).

Gathering evidence

CCTV recording can provide valuable evidence to link a gunman to a crime scene. Police investigators can spend a long time trawling through hours of CCTV footage back at the police station, looking for the crucial image.

As well as looking for the bullets themselves, investigators at the scene look for used cartridge cases, which can show where the shooter stood. Markings on the bullet can confirm what weapon was used, while the angle it hits a wall indicates where the gun was fired. All the evidence is sealed in plastic bags and after being photographed or videotaped, is sent to the crime laboratory.

ON TARGET

Though CCTV has great potential to detect gun crime, especially in banks and other enclosed spaces, one of its major drawbacks is that the operators often have to monitor many different cameras at once over long periods of time. At the moment a new software programme named MEDUSA is being developed that may help to detect someone carrying a gun or acting suspiciously. The software scans CCTV footage and looks for certain types of behaviour that suggest someone may be carrying a gun.

FIREARMS IN THE CRIME LAB

The first use of ballistics – working out the flight of a bullet – was by Joseph Bell, a 19th-century doctor who inspired fictional detective Sherlock Holmes. In gun crimes today, firearms examiners spend most of their time peering through powerful microscopes at tiny dents and scratches on bullets and cartridges which tell them what kind of gun was used.

Key evidence

At a crime scene, the victim's wounds, the bullets and gun are the key pieces of evidence. Fingerprints, blood splatters and fibres from clothing can also link the gun user to the scene, the gun or the victim. In a crime laboratory, forensic scientists test weapons and compare ammunition. Careful study of bullets and cartridges with a microscope and a computer matching system, along with tests done on a firing range, will usually identify which weapon was used. The FBI laboratory in Los Angeles has a large collection of weapons that can be used for comparison.

Comparing firearms

Gun records can give the background to a weapon recovered by the police. In the UK, the National Firearms Forensic Database provides a nationwide system for comparing firearms and ammunition recovered from crime scenes. Before the database was set up it could take several days to find a match between a particular weapon and other crimes. Now detectives can carry out a check in a few hours.

▼ *Many forensic scientists specialise in one area, such as firearms, blood splatters or fingerprints. Despite what you see on TV, forensic scientists don't interview anyone – they leave that to the detectives.*

▲ *A firearms officer discharging a pistol in a crime laboratory in Los Angeles, California, USA. Every gun leaves trademark marks and scratches on a bullet.*

Telltale signs

Lab technicians test a weapon for all sorts of clues to see if they match up to witness statements.

- To see if it may go off accidentally, if this is part of the shooter's defence.

- The spread of gunshot residue can show if someone was shot at very close range, often a sign of a gangland shooting rather than someone shooting in self-defence.

- If there is no gunshot residue on the victim's hands, it proves it was not a suicide and that the gun may have been planted in their hand after they were shot.

- Taking a weapon apart may also show if it has been converted from a fake into a real weapon.

ON TARGET

A new law in California, USA means that every semi-automatic handgun sold in the state will 'microstamp' each bullet cartridge in two places whenever it is fired. The stamp would identify the gun's make, model and serial number.

CASE STUDY:
THE WASHINGTON SNIPER

On 3 October 2002 an unknown gunman shot five people dead in 15 hours in a suburb of Washington, DC, USA. The next day the shootings continued, and a massive police operation was launched. Tracking down the killer was going to take a combination of good detective skills, forensics – and luck.

Fear and panic

A wave of fear quickly spread through the local community, mainly because there seemed no logic to the attacks. The first victim was shot dead in a grocery store car park, while others were shot mowing the lawn, filling a car with petrol or sitting on a bench. A few days later, a 13-year-old boy was shot outside his school. Though eyewitness accounts of the killings were confused, the evidence showed that most of the victims had been shot from long range, and the killer quickly became known as the 'Washington Sniper'.

Message from a killer

The sniper begun taunting the police with cryptic messages. He left tarot cards at several crime scenes, one with the message 'Dear Mr Police. Code: Call me God.' Later, the killer left handwritten notes demanding $10 million (£6.8 million). One ended with the chilling message: 'Your children are not safe anywhere or anytime.' As more people were shot, the police desperately searched for a clue that would help them track down the killer.

▼ Police officers prepare to search the parking lot where the sniper's tenth victim, FBI Intelligence Officer Linda Franklin, was found.

The breakthrough

The sniper rang the police and boasted of a previous attack in the town of Montgomery, Alabama. Police traced the call and rushed to the pay phone, but they missed the killer by just a few minutes. However, on 17 October they discovered that a fingerprint found at a previous shooting in Montgomery matched one found near the school in Washington where the 13-year-old boy had been murdered. The print belonged to a 17-year-old man called Lee Malvo.

Capture

Further detective work linked Malvo with another man John Allen Muhammed, the owner of a blue Chevrolet Caprice. Witnesses had reported seeing this car near several of the shootings. Finally, on 24 October, after the media informed the public about the Caprice, it was spotted in a highway rest area in the state of Maryland. The police found Malvo and Muhammed sleeping inside, along with a high-powered rifle. The police later matched the rifle to 11 of the 14 bullets found at earlier crime scenes. Muhammed was later found guilty of mass murder and executed on 10 November, 2009. Malvo was sentenced to life in prison for his role in the killings.

▼ *Suspect Lee Malvo is brought into court during the trial of sniper John Allen Muhammad.*

ON TARGET

The police realised they might have caught the two gunmen sooner if they had been able to match the sniper's bullets to those taken from the crime scene of the shooting in Montgomery. After the trial, a national database was set up to help local police forces match bullets with those in other states. Digital images allow bullets found at a crime scene to be matched to others in a few hours.

TACKLING GUN CRIME

Tighter gun control, better detective work and harsher prison sentences are all put forward as ways of tackling gun crime. Others argue that it can only be tackled effectively by dealing with the broader issues behind it such as poverty and drug abuse. While some violent criminals do have extreme personalities, many others are drawn into the gun culture by a lack of opportunity or a lack of education.

Guns and drugs

Gun crimes are often committed by criminal gangs with links to the drug trade. Enormous profits can be made quickly and gangs arm themselves to the teeth to protect their empires. A feud between rival drug gangs can soon turn into an arms race.

Police gang raids have uncovered weapons such as assault rifles, machine guns and grenade launchers. While there is so much money to be made from drugs, tighter gun control and increased prison sentences are unlikely to have any effect. Such gun crimes may only be stopped when it is no longer so profitable to deal in drugs.

▼ Traditionally, the Crips and Bloods crime gangs based in many US cities have been bitter enemies, often leading to open and bloody warfare on the streets. These gang members show their allegiance to the Bloods by wearing red (the Crips wear blue).

▲ *In Los Angeles, the annual Gun Buyback scheme encourages gun owners to exchange weapons for a grocery store gift card or a prepaid credit card. Some 2,500 firearms were collected in 2010.*

Community projects

In the United States, Project Safe Neighborhoods (PSN) aims to reduce gun and gang crime by funding local schemes that provide training, hand out gun lock safety kits and help to prevent troubled teenagers from getting drawn into the gun culture. The scheme recognises the fact that the reasons for gun crime are often different in different places and a local approach works better.

Firearms amnesty

Governments all over the world have tried to reduce the number of guns in their country with a firearms amnesty. In China, for instance, posters in subways ask people to hand in weapons to a local police station with no questions asked, or even for cash. A six month campaign in 2008 led to 79,000 guns, 1.8 million replicas and 5.75 million bullets being handed in.

ON TARGET

The British anti-gun crime charity the Disarm Trust was set up after two teenage girls were shot dead in Birmingham in 2003 during New Year celebrations. The trust works with local community groups in poor neighbourhoods where many young people have poor education and few job opportunities. They want to break the cycle of older criminals leading younger people into a life of crime, and prevent the spread of guns. The UK government helped to set up the charity using money recovered from convicted criminals.

CASE STUDY: OPERATION TRIDENT

Operation Trident is an anti-gun operation set up to help bring an end to a series of shootings and murders among young, black Londoners. It aims to tackle gun crime by working with community leaders and running high profile advertising campaigns aimed at encouraging young people to break away from the gun culture.

Police initiatives

Operation Trident was launched in July 2000 to deal with violent crimes in the London's black community, partly caused by the spread of the drug and turf wars between rival Jamaican, African and British-born gangs. The rise in gun crime in London has also been caused by easier access to weapons. A growing number of teenagers not linked to gangs have got involved in 'respect shootings' to settle petty arguments. There is an automatic 30-year prison sentence for murder, so a recent tactic has been to shoot victims in the leg to avoid killing them.

Vital evidence

Intelligence gathering is a very important part of the operation, but it is not easy as many gangs are divided into smaller units, each with their own names. As gang members have often known each other since school, it is also difficult to infiltrate them. Trident's advertising campaigns encourage people to phone in with information relating to gun crime. These adverts appear in newspapers, nightclubs, on petrol pumps, phone boxes and on the radio. One advert pointed out the dangers of carrying toy or imitation guns, while others highlight the brutal – and deadly – consequences of gun crime. However, even if people do phone in with good

▶ *This advert was designed by Operation Trident. It uses the simple children's game 'stone-paper-scissors' to encourage members of London's black community to phone in with information about gun crime.*

SCISSORS BEATS PAPER.

STONE BEATS SCISSORS.

PHONE BEATS GUN.

Stop the guns. Call Crimestoppers anonymously on 0800 555 111

TRIDENT

information, it can be very hard to get witnesses to stand up in court and testify. Critics of Trident say this is because there is not enough police protection and witnesses are too afraid of what will happen to them or their families if they give evidence.

The reality of gun crime

Operation Trident recognises that poor job prospects make it easy for drug gangs to tempt young people into crime by offering them large sums of money. It organises anti-gun talks for primary school children and teenagers where the speakers are often ex-criminals who don't want others to make the same mistakes they did. They explain to the audience the grim reality of spending 20 years in prison: 'No play stations, no Nintendo, hardcore jail where you've got someone telling you what to do, where to go, when to take a shower and when to go to bed.'

▼ Wayne Rowe (far right) is one of several reformed gang members who now work for Operation Trident. He talks to young people about the grim reality of gun crime and his experiences in prison.

BUSTED!

In June 2008 Operation Trident investigated the murder of 15-year-old Michael Dosunmu. The evidence given by six witnesses was key to the case. To protect their identities, the witnesses were hidden behind screens as they spoke, and three had their voices changed by computer technology so they could not be recognised. When witnesses don't come forward, technology and painstaking detective work can help. In March 2005, two young men were convicted of the murder of Letisha Shakespeare and Charlene Ellis (see p.35) outside a hair salon in Birmingham in 2003, thanks to detailed mobile phone evidence that tied them to the murder scene.

GUN CRIME IN THE MEDIA

Many argue that the media is a bad influence on people's attitudes to gun and gun crime. Films often feature guns and shoot-outs, glamorising guns and making extreme violence seem normal. Meanwhile, news reports of murders and other violent crimes can make ordinary people afraid, even though their chances of being affected by gun crime are relatively slim.

A powerful allure

Films, TV shows and violent computer games help to glorify the gun – the gunman is often made to look cool or in control, while carrying a gun is made to seem the most natural thing in the world. As a result, guns have a powerful appeal, even if they are never used. Gang members often wear them as a symbol of their deadly power and revel in the fear they inspire in their victims and enemies.

▼ *James Bond, licensed to kill. Films and TV programmes have long glamorised guns, but the reality of gun crime is brutal, shocking and tragic.*

Is there a link?

In some police shows, shots are fired in every other scene and deaths are common. By the time the average American child reaches the age of 18, they have witnessed 16,000 murders and 200,000 acts of violence on screen. However, after 50 years and hundreds of different studies, scientists cannot agree whether there is a direct link between violence on screen and violence in real life. Though TV shows can make violence seem normal and do make some children more aggressive, there are many other reasons why violent crimes are committed.

▲ One of the criticisms of video games is that they make people more violent. But most studies show this is only true when that person is naturally aggressive and/or is having other problems at home or at school.

Gun crime in the news

Real-life crime stories grab people's attention and sell newspapers. As a result, violent crimes, especially murders, often get a lot of coverage. As a result of this, it can sometimes seem that gun crime is a lot more prevalent than it really is. Some journalists make the point that reporting murders is important as it reinforces the point that killing is wrong and shocking. Others argue that there is demand from the public to feature crime stories. But along with this interest comes the element of fear, which can encourage people to own a weapon to defend themselves. Ironically those least likely to be victims of crime are those likely to be most afraid – the elderly – while those most at risk – young men – are least likely to worry.

▶ Hip-hop stars such as NWA, Snoop Dogg and T.I. (right) have been criticised for glamorising guns in their lyrics. They claim they are just reflecting real life on the streets.

BUSTED!

Rap music with violent and aggressive language has also been blamed for encouraging gun crime and glamorising gangs. In its defence, some argue that films and computer games glorify guns far more than music and there are more important causes of violent crime. However, rap's violent image wasn't helped when US hip-hop star T.I. was convicted in May 2009 after FBI agents found his car contained several machine guns and his jacket was stuffed with bullets. They also discovered a weapons store at his home including a laser-sighted sniper's rifle.

AN ONGOING DEBATE

The debate over gun laws remains a hot topic in many countries. While some politicians campaign for tighter controls, gun enthusiasts refuse to give up their arms. As a result, gun control laws vary wildly even within one country. In US cities such as New York or Chicago it is difficult or impossible to legally keep guns for self-defence, while in other parts of the United States, the gun laws are very relaxed.

◀ Guns are deadly. When they get into the wrong hands, the outcome can be devastating. Australian Martin John Bryant murdered 35 people and injured 21 after he went on a shooting spree in Port Arthur, Tasmania in 1996.

ON TARGET

Some experts argue that gun manufacturers should be forced to adopt 'smart gun' technology to help prevent gun crime. In future, all guns could be computerised with special sensors that would prevent anyone except the owner of the gun from using it.

Variations in the law

Some countries are creating tighter gun controls. Australia, for example, introduced new laws after the Port Arthur massacre in 1996 which killed 35 people.There has also been a campaign in Australia by police and shooting organisations to encourage gun owners to make sure their weapons are kept under lock and key. This has led to a big reduction in the number of stolen weapons. In the United Kingdom, anyone caught carrying a replica gun in public gets an automatic five-year jail sentence. Meanwhile some states in the United States have been heading in the opposite direction. In 2005 Florida introduced a law allowing citizens the right to 'stand their ground' and open fire even in a public place if they feel threatened.

Working with gun owners

Some argue, however, that it's almost impossible to outlaw guns – there are just too many of them around already. They want the police to work with gun clubs to clamp down on the black market for weapons, which supplies many of the criminal gangs. Gun enthusiasts are often aware of the gun shops that will sell to anyone. The Boston Gun Project in the United States has been very successful in tackling gun crime by targeting dealers who sold guns that ended up in the hands of criminals.

What's the future?

Gun crime remains a problem for many countries. In the United Kingdom, after many years without mass shootings, a gun spree by taxi driver Derrick Bird in June 2010 re-opened the gun laws debate. Despite the arguments, few would disagree that new ways need to be found of preventing gun crime, whether by gun control, better detective methods, working with local communities or dealing with the bigger related issues such as drugs and poverty.

ON TARGET

Police and law enforcement agencies have teamed up in a new anti-gun crime programme in the US city of Minneapolis after the homicide rate there rose dramatically in 2010. The plan will bring in longer sentences for criminals who use and sell guns. In particular, the team hope to clamp down on people who buy guns then sell them on to criminals.

▲ The British police force is one of the few in the world where officers do not routinely carry guns. But the rise of violent crime in London and the threat from terrorists has led to more armed police officers on the city's streets.

GLOSSARY

Assassin A murderer who targets a particular victim, often an important person, and kills them in a surprise attack. Assassins are often paid to kill.

Automatic weapon A gun that reloads itself and keeps firing until the trigger is released.

Ballistics The study of flying bullets.

Black market Buying something, such as a gun, from an illegal source.

Bulletproof Making something, such as a car window or door, strong enough to stop a bullet.

Bystander Someone who is at a crime scene but who does not take part. Bystanders are often important witnesses. They can also get hit in gun battles between the police and criminals.

CCTV Closed-circuit television, a system that uses video cameras to keep watch on a particular place, often found in banks, airports and jewellery stores.

CS gas A gas used by police to control riots or violent suspects. Effects include tears streaming from the eyes, coughing, dizziness and vomiting.

DNA (deoxyribonucleic acid) The main molecule that holds genetic information in living things.

Drug cartel An organisation that controls the production, supply and sale of illegal drugs.

FBI (Federal Bureau of Investigation) US government security service responsible for solving crimes.

Firearm A gun such as a handgun, shotgun or rifle.

Forensics Scientific tests or techniques used to investigate crimes.

Gun control Laws created to control the sale of guns.

Gun culture How guns are used in society. It is much more common to own a gun in some countries than in others.

Gun rights groups Groups that believe people have a right to own or carry guns.

Gun shows An exhibition where firearms and ammunition are bought and sold.

Handgun A firearm with a short barrel usually used with one hand, such as a pistol or revolver.

Homicide A murder or illegal death caused by another person.

Killing spree When a murderer kills two or more victims in a short space of time.

Licence A permit, for example to own a gun.

Machine gun A rapidly firing automatic weapon.

Massacre When lots of people are killed at the same time, usually in a violent way.

Militia People who have trained as soldiers but are not part of a regular army.

Reasonable force Also called legal force, this means the amount of force a person or police officer can use to protect themselves while staying within the law.

Replica A copy. Replica guns are sometimes used by criminals in a robbery. They can also be adapted to fire real bullets.

Rifle A long-barrelled gun that fires bullets. The grooves or rifling along its barrel help the bullet to travel in a straight line. It is designed for use at long range.

Semi-automatic A firearm that fires a single shot and reloads each time the trigger is pulled.

Serial killer Someone who murders more than three victims in separate incidents, in a short space of time.

Shoot-to-kill A policy of killing dangerous suspects without trying to arrest or question them.

Shotgun A gun with a smooth barrel that fires shot (small metal balls).

Sniper A marksman who shoots at people from a concealed place, often at long range.

Trafficking Smuggling illegal goods, especially drugs.

Vigilante Someone who takes the law into their own hands. Vigilantes punish criminals themselves rather than going to the police.

FURTHER INFORMATION

Books

Angela Royston, *Gun Crimes (Solve It With Science)*, Franklin Watts, 2009

Chris Cooper, *Forensic Science*, Dorling Kindersley, 2008

Websites

www.fbi.gov/fbikids.htm
The kid's section of the Federal Bureau of Investigation website allows young people to learn more about the FBI through games, stories and interactives. It also shows how FBI agents and analysts investigate serious crimes.

www.soca.gov.uk
The website of the Serious Organised Crime Agency describes how SOCA fights serious crime in the UK, including gun crime and drug crime.

www.met.police.uk/history/flying_squad.htm
A history of the famous Metropolitan Police Flying Squad.

natgeotv.com/uk/flying-squad
Video footage showing Flying Squad in action.

people.howstuffworks.com/street-gang.htm
A website looking at street gangs and gun violence.

Note to parents and teachers: every effort has been made by the Publishers to ensure that these websites are suitable for children, that they are of the highest educational value, and that they contain no inappropriate or offensive material. However, because of the nature of the Internet, it is impossible to guarantee that the contents of these sites will not be altered. We strongly advise that Internet access is supervised by a responsible adult.

INDEX

SERIES CONTENTS